Prayer Arsenal:

Weapons to Defeat the Enemy

Revised Version

To Pastor Johnson,
May God continue
to bless & increase
you in every
good work
in Jesus' name !

Shana-Kay and Gary Granville

Publishers - Shana-Kay & Gary Granville
Graphic Designer - Jae-Anne Willie-Belle
Editors - Nathan Patrick PhD, Gary Granville and Shana-Kay Granville, JWG Publishing
Authors' Photo - Terrell Scudder

For more copies of this book, please email graceondemandministries@gmail.com

ISBN 978-1-5323-8846-0
Printed in the United States of America

Foreword

Christians are constantly in warfare of some sort on a daily basis. The battles we face as Christians take place in the spiritual realm. In order to fully understand these battles, we must acknowledge that we are unceasingly in warfare. In warfare, battles are fought from unprecedented angles, for divergent reasons and with varying degrees of intensity. The same is quite true in spiritual warfare. As believers, our battles and warfare are perceptible and even though we cannot physically see our opponents or attackers, we are cognizant that we are constantly engaging in spiritual battles.

This revised version of Prayer Arsenal provides the foundation upon which Christians can become victorious in their everyday battle. It undoubtedly purveys a valuable window on how victory is achieved in spiritual warfare through the power of the Holy Ghost. This wonderful book can be a treasured resource for all Christians. This revised version unfolds an amazing story of how to better educate and equip ourselves on how battles are fought and how they undoubtedly impact our day to day lives as believers. What Gary and Shana-Kay have done is to write a book that is not only original but also one that is interesting and impactful. This material will prove tremendously helpful to Christians as they prepare for warfare. What strikes me most about their work is the brevity and practicality they conjure in presenting to believers in the body of Christ, some useful, practical and insightful approaches on how to fight spiritual warfare effectively and live victorious lives.

I can assure you that the experience you will gain from reading Prayer Arsenal will be very gratifying as the authors present their book with great originality and clearly articulate some useful and effective prayer points after each chapter that afford readers the opportunity to develop greater skills in combating warfare. I am indeed humbled and grateful to have met Gary and Shana-Kay Granville.

To me, it was a divine connection that brought us together. I can unequivocally state without reservations that this book is a must read as it puts forward a sagacious and irrepressible master plan. It will endow believers to become empowered and equipped to combat the enemy by undermining his strategies and live victorious lives, and so I am immensely grateful for their publication of Prayer Arsenal: Weapons to Defeat the Enemy.

Bishop Dr. Reckonel Simpson, EdD
College Professor and Motivational Speaker
Kingston, Jamaica

CONTENTS

<u>Objective</u>

The aim of this book is to:

- ☐ To give you a better understanding of your role as a Christian soldier.
- ☐ To outline the importance of wearing the Armor of God.
- ☐ To make you aware of different types of spiritual weapons.
- ☐ To expand your knowledge as you study the scripture.
- ☐ To improve your prayer life by praying at a higher dimension.
- ☐ To challenge you to believe God for a positive outcome.

This book is not a *formula for answered prayers or a* guarantee that all prayers will be answered how you expect them to!

Every believer has a responsibility to live godly and to believe God for that which they are seeking after. You receive only to the extent to which you believe and exercise your faith. Allow the Holy Spirit to lead and pray through you! Also, remember that God only works on His timing and His agenda.

2 Corinthians 13:5 (NASB)

Test yourselves to see if you are in the faith; examine yourselves! Or do you not recognise this about yourselves that Jesus Christ is in you-- unless indeed you fail the test?

2 Samuel 22:21 (KJV)

The LORD rewarded me according to my righteousness: according to the cleanness of my hands hath he recompensed me

Introduction

The body of Christ is being called to new levels of spiritual warfare. We must be sure to remember that our fight is never with people. The Bible reminds us in the book of Ephesians 6:12 (NLT) that we are not fighting against flesh-and-blood, but against evil rulers and authorities of the unseen world, against mighty powers in this dark world, and against evil spirits in the heavenly places. Principalities, powers, rulers and wickedness operating in the second heaven, have strategically positioned themselves in regions, countries, organizations and communities to override God's plan for humanity and execute Satan's agenda.

The moment you enter into a relationship with Jesus Christ, the battle begins. The moment you strive for spiritual maturity, the battles intensify even more, and you become a high prized target on the devil's hit list. The enemy has launched his attack on our spirits, souls, bodies, ministry, marriage, family, health, finances, and the list goes on. Regardless of your religious background: Catholic, Methodist, Anglican, Seventh Day Adventist, Pentecostal, Presbyterian, etc., the enemy will come after you with vengeance so be ready!

Some time ago, Lord used me to empower a former colleague, who I will refer to as Marie. Marie was raised in a Seventh Day Adventist church. A thing to note is that Seventh Day Adventists do not believe in the baptism of the Holy Ghost, spiritual warfare, or demons. The more I engaged her on the subject of spiritual warfare and deliverance, the more her interest grew. You could see the sorrow (for the lack of information because of her affiliation) and the desperation of wanting more of God each time we talked on the subject. I shared my testimonies and explain how generational curses and witchcraft practices can prevent people from coming into their God-given purpose. We talked for days. I loaned her books and sent her YouTube videos. Today I am happy to report that she is a radical warrior for God in the Seventh Day Adventist Church; but more importantly, she is a warrior in God's army. God is looking for a remnant in these last days that is radical and not afraid to expose, tackle, and defeat satanic devices.

St. John 10:10 list Satan's primary objectives. These are to steal, kill and to destroy. Luke 18:1 reminds us that men must always pray and not faint. Today too many Christians are collapsing because of unbelief and a lack of cultivating the fruit of the Spirit: many today are in need of an abundance of patience. We have to rid ourselves of this "fainting spell". It short-circuits the anointing, and it prevents the believer from living the abundant life that Christ promised. Many Christians enter spiritual warfare unprepared, and lack of preparation can result in a severe casualty!

In the physical world, a soldier needs to be prepared for war at all times, they do so by constantly training and learning new tactics. They engage in war games, which is a dress rehearsal for the real thing: they cannot afford go to war unprepared. They have to be clothed in the proper uniforms and have the right weapons available at their disposal. Likewise, in the body Christ a soldier must wear the whole armour of God. Ephesians 6:11 (CEV) tells us, "put on all the armour that God gives so that you can defend yourself against the devil's tricks." And be fully aware of the weapons available.

Please note that the Bible does not mention at anytime, that we should ever take it off. We will look in detail at the armor of God in the chapter, "Dressed for Battle. For now, I want us to focus on this fact. God needs trained, equip and ready warriors in His ranks to carry out His plans here on earth!

This book is for Christians who have little or no knowledge about spiritual warfare. It is for those who will dare to answer the call and fight in prayer for their families, church, community and country. It is for the man or woman of God that has decided to engage the enemy without fear; it is for those that have fully trusted Jesus Christ our Lord and want to carry on the mission of setting God's people free.

The prayer at the end of each chapter is an example of how to use these weapons in warfare type prayers. You are also required to complete the assignment as this will help you to get in the habit of developing prayer points (areas of focus for strategic prayer). In spiritual warfare, practicality is required. In being practical, it is imperative that you grow in the Word. When you know and understand the Word of God, your prayer life will take on a new dimension.

My prayer is that you will arise, take up your weapons and fight the good fight of faith.

The Revelation

One day while heading to church with my family, the Holy Spirit stirred me to pray. An unusual anointing came upon me and I knew that God wanted my attention. As I yielded myself to the move of the Holy Spirit, the Lord showed me evil words released into the atmosphere against me and my family. I began to call forth spiritual weapons to appear as the Lord directed me. As I called them into existence, I would use each of them to destroy a specific device that the Lord was revealing to me. Note carefully that the moment an evil word is released into the atmosphere demons are assigned to ensure that they manifest. Immediately after I finished praying, I sensed a breakthrough in the atmosphere.

After this revelation, I began to study the scriptures. During my studies, the Holy Spirit revealed to me the Biblically soundness for what I saw that morning while heading to church. This is why it is essential to stay connected to the Lord our God. He is a revealer of the secret things, and He protects His children from the enemy. He has also made an arsenal of spiritual weapons available and when use properly and consistently; they will defeat our enemy at every turn.

The arsenal of God belongs to the believers. It is there for us to access in times of need and wage warfare against the enemy of our destiny. No army exists without an arsenal. An arsenal is a collection of weapons and equipment stored up by a fighting force. The military uses weapons such as grenades, handguns, rifles, shotguns, machine guns, tanks, jets, etc. These are used to disarm their enemies, whether by injury or death. The army of God also has an arsenal. These weapons, when appropriately used, enable us to defeat the enemy. However, we have to become experts in using them. Many Christians are not aware of the fact that they have a spiritual arsenal available to them to combat the enemy. The physical world, in which we live and operate, is a reflection of the spiritual one. Matthew 18:18 (KJV) tells us, "Verily I say unto you; whatsoever ye shall bind on earth shall be bound in heaven: and whatsoever ye shall loose on earth shall be loosed in heaven." Before actively engaging our weaponry, we must ensure that we are properly dressed for battle.

Dressed for Battle

In the book of Ephesians, the apostle Paul listed weapons and pieces of armor that believers should be dressed in when engaging the enemy of our souls. Paul's illustration came from observing the most potent fighting force of his day, the Roman army. The Roman army was a disciplined, well trained, and well-equip fighting force. They were very ruthless towards their enemies and employed some of the most brilliant military tactics, which we still study and marvel at today. Paul also indicated that our enemy is very organized and motivated in his pursuit to destroy the body of Christ. As Christians, we must be organized and discipline in our defense of the Gospel of Jesus Christ. Remember this; we are fighting from a victorious position. Jesus Christ our Lord has already overcome the wicked one! As Paul changed the subject in verse 10 of Ephesians chapter 6, he calls the believer to something that Roman soldiers knew well to do: to be strong and stand your ground. The Christian soldier should always stand their ground and be strong in the power of God's

Spirit, *"be strong in the Lord and the power of His might" (Eph 6:10 KJV)*.

We cannot stand in our power or our strength. Even though Jesus was God in humanity, He always relied on the Father for everything and in every situation. We must be aware that the tactics the devil employs are born out of confusion, deceit, and lies. Paul indicated that being secure in Jesus Christ and putting on His whole armour is the only way we are going to be able to withstand the wiles of the devil. *According to dictionary.com the word "wiles" is a "trick, artifice, or stratagem meant to fool, trap, or entice"*. The same dictionary defines withstand this way, *"to stand or hold out against; resist or oppose, especially successfully"*. Take a minute to examine your Christian walk and I'm sure you will find this to be true in how the enemy attacks you. He uses tricks and deceptive schemes to fool us into believing his lies. The question we need to answer individually is this. Are we holding out against him and doing so successfully?

BELT OF TRUTH

Paul indicates that if we are to be strong in the Lord then our Christian stance firstly must be held together by the truth. *"So stand firm and hold your ground, having tightened the wide band of truth (personal integrity, moral courage) around your waist" (Eph. 6:14a AMP).* It is no coincident that the apostle started with loins, the loins represent a person's seat of strength and vigour. This region between the lowest ribs and the top part of the pelvis (both sides of the spine) is also seen as a man's centre of procreative power; in many cultures around the world. Therefore, wearing a belt around this area gave it additional strength and signifies that person wearing this belt is ready for service or a great endeavour. Just as in ancient times, people use such special belts for heavy lifting or intense manual work today.

The loins of our spirit man needs the truth of God's Word for this type of fortification. As we engage in spiritual battles, only God's truth will give us the strength to stand and resist the advances and attacks of the enemy. The belt of truth is also an anchor for other weapons such as the breastplate of righteousness and the sword of the Spirit. No spiritual endeavor can be successful without girding one's self with the truth and no spiritual being will recognize you as ready if you are not girded with the truth!

BREASTPLATE OF RIGHTEOUSNESS

"...and having put on the breastplate of righteousness (an upright heart)," (Ep. 6: 14b AMP). Uprightness of heart is one of the believer's most potent defensive weapons. The Bible tells us that the devil is like a roaring lion seeking whom he may devour. Let us think about this for a while. What exactly is Satan searching for when he prowls around systematically examining each area of our lives? The answer is simply a weakness; he is looking for an entry, something that will give his attack potency and effectiveness in the believer's life.

He is looking for a flaw that he can agree with, something that will justify the attack and give it the legal footing to stay. That weakness, brethren, is SIN. When Satan launches his attacks on a believer, he is very methodical about it. He doesn't just go at it in a frenzied manner, he is very deliberate in what he is doing. Therefore, we must ensure that we fortify our lives with the Word of God, standing on the righteousness that is by faith in Christ alone.

The Bible tells us that, " ...*the curse without cause does not come and alight [on the undeserving];" (Proverbs 26: 2 AMP)*. Jesus echoed a similar sentiment in the New Testament when he stated, *"...for the ruler of the world (Satan) is coming. And he has no claim on me [no power over me nor anything that he can use against me];" (John 14:30 AMP)*. When we as believers live in sin or don't confess our sins to the Lord, we are giving the devil a claim over us and power over us to some extent. Creating the weakness, he needs to deliver a severe blow.

On the contrary, by living upright before the Lord, we are giving the Holy Spirit free reign to encircle us with His protective fire. I am not saying we will not fail or make mistakes. We will, but when we do, we must quickly repent and turn to the Lord, so we can stay within the cover of His righteousness; ensuring that the integrity of our breastplate remains intact. Remember as Christians, we must always strive to live a life that is pleasing to Jesus Christ, our King, relying entirely on the Holy Spirit. Again, uprightness in heart believers is a great protective weapon!

GOSPEL OF PEACE

The best news in the world is Jesus Christ paid the debt for all our sins, removing those that trust in Him from under the wrath of God. So " *having [c]strapped on your feet the gospel of peace in preparation [to face the enemy with firm-footed stability and the readinessproduced by the good news," (Ep. 6: 15 AMP).* Let us move forward with the assurance that we stand on His promises, spreading the hope to as many as we can for as long as we can! Often the devil uses the tactic of questioning our salvation; casting doubts in our minds about the pardon, we freely received from the Lord. This occurs especially when we fall after resisting the restraining power of the Holy Spirit. Our enemy inflicts us with guilt and condemnation, which can lead to depression and despair.

When we have, our feet strapped with the gospel of peace we can. **1**-walk in the assurance that Jesus Christ our Lord has fully and freely pardoned our sins (past, present, and future) once we confess. When we fail, our status in Him is not taken away or lost. **2**-confidently share His love and peace with others, thereby fulfilling His command of making disciples of all nations.

SHIELD OF FAITH

When fighting wars, commanders are always aware of the need to protect their troops. In our world today, armies invest heavily in protective armor, such as tanks etc. In ancient Rome, soldiers mainly used a shield as part of their protective armor. They mainly used two types: a small round shield used for parading and in one-on-one combat, and a big rectangular one used in huge campaigns. The rectangular shield was almost as tall as a soldier was.

Roman soldiers trained extensively to use these individually and collectively. Roman legions had military formations that required soldiers to interlock shields. Are you locking faith with believers in your sphere? In verse 16 of Ephesians 6, Paul tells us that…" *above all, lift up the [protective]* [d]*shield of faith with which you can extinguish all the flaming arrows of the evil one.*" in the days of Roman conquest, defenders of cities would often shoot fiery arrows on advancing legions. To counter this, the soldiers of Rome would dip their shields in water and olive oil to moisten the leather covering. This would make the shield resistant to burn when hit by one of these fiery arrows. While engaging the devil we would be in serious trouble if we for one reason or another let down our shield. Our shield consisting of faith in Christ must be in the correct position at all times. Christians must stand individually in faith in many situations and circumstances, but often times we are required to stand collectively faith. The devil fights us very fiercely and aggressively, especially when we are advancing on his strongholds. When he launches his arrows, he is serious. We, therefore, must lift and keep lifting our shield of faith.

The Bible tells us that faith is the substance of things hoped for, the evidence of things not seen. As believers, we must stand on the promises that God has given to us through His written and spoken Word. What is the devil firing at you? Is it sticking and burning away at your Christian walk? If yes, you must raise your shield of faith to counter this ploy and regain the advantage that Christ has given to you.

HELMET OF SALVATION

"And take the helmet of salvation, and the sword of the Spirit, which is the Word of God", (Eph. 6:17 AMP). It is not peculiar that Paul would use the

phrase "helmet of salvation" and rightly so. One of the most significant advantages a Christian has is knowledge. It is not the knowledge of know of someone or something, but the knowledge of being intimate with someone or something. For the believer this knowledge is the comprehension and heartfelt appreciation our salvation was secured through the atoning blood of Jesus Christ and that we are standing firm in the truth. The helmet of salvation is the covering that protects the seat of our understanding. Once we as believers have a healthy spiritual understanding of what Jesus Christ did for us at Calvary and continues to do for us at the Father's right hand, we will be able to resist the devil's attempts to sow doubts and fears about our standing with God. This leads me to the next point, our thought process or way of thinking is very critical to how we live. Most things that we see around us was first in someone's mind. If the devil can infiltrate our thought processes and get us to accept his lies, then he can control our movements a great deal. The helmet of salvation is the defensive weapon that we must use to protect our thoughts. Don't allow Satan to overwhelm you with his evil thoughts and tell you who you are. Remember the truth of salvation is you were bought with the precious blood of Jesus Christ, and you are who God says you are. Whenever he attacks your mind, manoeuvre the helmet of salvation to take and defuse the blows just as a Roman soldier would against projectiles aimed at his head.

THE SWORD OF THE SPIRIT

The sword of the Spirit is both an offensive and defensive weapon. In a one-on-one duel with an enemy combatant, a Roman soldier would have to both block the incoming blows by skillfully using both his sword and shield. While doing this, he would also look for weaknesses in his enemy and try to exploit them with his sword. When a Roman legion advanced and held a line, the sword of each soldier was also employed collectively in that formation. For each configuration of a legion, the sword of each legionnaire in the ranks came together against their enemies with deadly accuracy. When a Roman army moved across a battlefield, usually no enemy soldier was spared, especially those that resisted any demands before the conflict. As believers, we also must be skilled in using our sword, the Word of God. The Word of God is our sword, and to accurately use it we must study and correctly apply it. When Jesus faced the devil in the wilderness, He employed the Word skillfully in both a defensive and offensive manner to defeat Satan's attempts to overcome Him. Only the believer with a deep spiritual appreciation for the Word will get the advantage over the devil.

The spiritual weapons outlined by Paul show that we, as believers, will always be frequently engaged in close or hand-to-hand combat with the devil and his hosts. The Holy Spirit revealed to me, however, that the strength of Satan and his hosts when they get near enough for close or hand-to-hand combat is dependent on how we use the other weapons described throughout the scriptures (God's arsenal of spiritual weapons). In the coming chapters, we will look at some other spiritual armaments talked about in the Bible. As believers we must use these weapons from God's arsenal to hit the enemy from a distance; just as a Roman legion would use their ***arrows, spears, javelins, battering rams (hammer), giant catapults*** etc. to take the main sting out of an enemy's attack or to weaken their defences.

Understanding Spiritual Authority

Recently, I went through a major crisis in my life. I disobeyed the Holy Spirit, and that opened the door for the enemy to attack my mind; my wife was going through a major battle, or should I say, was coming to the ending of one. She would often tell me during this instance of testing that I needed to understand my identity in Christ. She would stress the point every time she encouraged me. Once I got over the attack of Satan on my life, the Holy Spirit gave me a revelation of who I am in Jesus Christ as well as the authority that I possess through Him. This revelation catapulted me into a new dimension in my walk with the Lord and the execution of my God-given assignment.

Many Christians today are faced with this very same identity crisis of not knowing who they are in Christ. As a result of this lack of knowledge, they lead defeated lives. The abundant life that Christ promises seems to elude them, and countless populace dies without fully realizing their God-given purpose in the earth realm.

"Behold, I give unto you power to tread on serpents and scorpions, and over all the power of the enemy: and nothing shall by any means hurt you", (Luke 10:19 KJV).

The word "power" here means authority. Authority according to dictionary.com is defined as

"The power to determine, adjudicates, or otherwise settle issues or disputes" jurisdiction; the right to control, command, or determine".

Let us dissect this for a moment and look at what Jesus Christ our Lord is saying to His people.

The power to determine - God has given each believer the right to decide what happens within his or her sphere. If something is happening in that area that does not align with the Word of God, you and I have the power to determine its fate. If it succeeds, it is because we have allowed it. If it does not, it is because we precluded it.

Adjudicate - Through Christ Jesus, our Lord we have the power to issue a judgment within the natural and supernatural realms, just as how a judge would work in our legal systems here on earth. Our Heavenly Father sits as the only Supreme Court Justice of the universe, we as His

children sit as circuit court judges, and we are mandated to administer and enforce His law. If say, for example, the spirit of infirmity attacks our health we can override that assignment by the Word of God, condemning that scheme to failure.

Otherwise, settle issues or disputes – What are the conflicts that are now presently working against you or your church? What are the problems of life that are far contrary to your God-given call and assignment or that of your ministry or church? Jesus Christ is saying to you and me, through His Word, that we have the power to settle those issues and resolve every dispute.

Jurisdiction- *"and let them have dominion over the fish of the sea, and over the fowl of the air, and over the cattle, and over all the earth, and over every creeping thing that creepeth upon the earth"*, *(Gen. 1:26).*

As believers, we have authority in the earth realm. *"And hath raised us up together, and made us sit together in heavenly places in Christ Jesus"*: *(Eph.*

2:6). As believers, we have authority in the spiritual realm.

The right to control, command, or determine *–Being* soldiers in Christ we have the power to control, to steer, to direct things in our here. We can command and veto items in our sphere. We can determine where, when, and how things should unfold.

It is essential to know that exercising one's God-given authority is very critical in spiritual warfare. If we are ignorant of this, then we won't be able to efficiently utilize the spiritual weapons Jesus Christ has made available to us in His Word. Now that you are aware that God has given us authority, we can wage war on behalf of God's kingdom effectively. Next, we will delve deeper into the following weapons in God's arsenal made available to every one of His sons and daughters.

Weapon # 1 - The Hammer of God

Weapon # 2 – The Axe of God

Weapon # 3 – The Sword of the Spirit

Weapon # 4 – The Breath of God

Weapon # 5 – The Finger of God

Weapon # 6 – The Right Hand of God

Weapon # 7 - The Wind of God

Weapon # 8 – The Arrow of God

Weapon # 9 – The Lightning & Thunder of God

Weapon # 10 – The Fire of God

Weapon # 11 - The Hailstones of God

Weapon # 12 - The Earthquake of the Lord

Weapon # 13 – The Blood of Jesus Christ

The Hammer of God

A hammer is a tool with a dense metal head used to break apart, weaken an object, and drive nails. It is usually placed on a solid wood or metal cylindrical beam. Depending on the type, the beam might be long or short. One of the biggest hammers ever employed was the battering ram. In medieval times and during the Roman conquest, invading armies would use it in war campaigns called sieges to conquer a region. To defeat an area these armies would have to take the main fortifications. This was significant because nobles and kings used forts in the form of castles and strongholds to hold and defend their territories.

Trained soldiers would take the battering ram to the main gates of the stronghold, which was under heavy guard. When in position it was used, as the name suggests, to batter the entry until it was demolished. The defending forces would try to prevent this by throwing rocks, pouring boiling oil, and shooting fiery arrows at the invaders operating this machinery.

When Satan invades one's life, he establishes strongholds to hold "territories" in our soul. It is from these areas he launch attacks into other areas. Let me break it down further for you, if Satan captures your sexuality through pornography, he then launches raids into your marriage. Before you know it, he becomes a resident. His ultimate goal is to destroy you, doing so piece by piece.

The Hammer of God is the weapon from the arsenal that we employ to break down satanic strongholds in our lives. Without the eradication of these forts and the demonic spirits that operate them, we will never be free. The following prayer points give an example of how we can employ the Hammer of God (His battering ram) against satanic strongholds in our lives. These prayer points were derived from the two scriptural references below.

PRAYER POINTS

Jeremiah 23:29 (KJV)

"Is not my word like as a fire? Saith the LORD; *and like a hammer that breaketh the rock in pieces?"*

Jeremiah 51:20-23 (ESV)

"You are my hammer and weapon of war: with you I break nations in pieces; with you I destroy kingdoms; with you, I break in pieces the horse and his rider; with you, I break in pieces the chariot and the charioteer; with you I break in pieces man and woman; with you I break in pieces the old man and the youth; with you I break in pieces the young man and the young woman; with you I break in pieces the shepherd and his flock; with you I break in pieces the farmer and his team;

with you I break in pieces governors and commanders."

Father, in the name of Jesus Christ I call forth the hammer of God to break in pieces every rejection, anger, and curses trailing me through my family's bloodline. Hammer of God; dismantle foundational problems and strongholds that hinder the free flow of your blessings upon my life. I use the hammer of God to smash the head of every serpentine spirit hissing away at my success. Father use me to breakdown every satanic altar that has been erected to stop my progress. God use me as your hammer (battering ram) and break to pieces marital problems, destroy kingdoms of financial lack in my life in the name of Jesus!

Break in pieces the horse and rider that interferes with my mind. Almighty God, by You I break in pieces chariots riding away with my blessings. By you Lord, I break in pieces every human spirit that wants to sabotage my breakthrough!

By you God, I break in pieces every spirit that acts as a gatekeeper in my life in Jesus name! By you Lord, I break in pieces every deadbolt, shackle, chain and fetters of iron that the enemy has placed upon me. I command you to break in pieces by the hammer

of God! Release your hold in my life in Jesus name.
Amen!

ASSIGNMENT

Study the scripture references. Write down your own prayer points using the Hammer of God.

_____

_____

_____

_____

_____

_____

_____

_____

_____

_____

_____

_____

_____

_____

_____

_____

_____

_____

_____

_____

The Axe of God

An axe is a wedged metal attached to a wooden or metallic handle. It is used mostly to chop wood. Today it is also used by firefighters and rescue teams to break down barriers, etc. We often don't hear the term battle axe in our times, but during the days of Paul this would be a common term, especially among persons in the military. When the Roman legions attacked barbaric tribes, the battle-axe was a weapon of choice. These range in size and design. Persons using battle-axes would be trained to use the weapon from an early age and for a variety of application. In the movie, *Braveheart,* some of the men fighting with the main protagonist, William Wallace, played by Mel Gibson, wielded battle-axes.

The *Battle of Stirling* scene is a very graphic example of the effectiveness of this weapon in the hand of a skilled fighter. In modern times, an axe is mainly used to chop wood, especially in rural areas. In both urban and rural areas, emergency services use axes to break down doors and barriers that block them in emergencies. Firefighters and search and rescue teams have this tool as part of their gear.

When a firefighter has to rescue someone, he has no time for finesse. Lives are at stake, and any barrier that prevents the execution of his mission will meet his axe. Think about your loved ones that are barricaded behind Satanic lies and deceptions. They are in need of rescuing. If they are delivered, they might be pushed further into their condition, ending up in destruction. You have to use the Axe of God to break down those barriers and rescue those in danger. There is no time to waste! Pick up your spiritual axe and begin to break through those obstacles that stand in the way of those who need deliverance!

John told the Pharisees that the axe was already at their roots, and that God would remove every tree that is not bearing good fruit. If you have "trees" in your life that are producing bad attitudes, mediocre results, and the works of the flesh, the Axe of the Lord is needed to cut them down. Who is the Satanic strongman that is now squaring off with you? Ask the Holy Spirit to give you the skill and prowess to cut them down.

PRAYER POINTS

Matthew 3:10 (NASB)

"The axe is already laid at the root of the trees; therefore every tree that does not bear good fruit is cut down and thrown into the fire."

Ezekiel 26:9 (NASB)

"The blow of his battering rams he will direct against your walls, and with his axes, he will break down your towers."

Father, I acknowledge that you are a man of war. The Lord is your name according to Exodus 15: 3. I call forth the Axe of God in the name of Jesus Christ. Almighty Father, give me the skill right now to use the Axe of God to lay it at the root of the trees of stubborn problems in my life. The spirit of financial handicap, lack, poverty, sickness, depression, frustration, unforgiveness, pride, and divorce. You are not bearing good fruit in my life, I lay the Axe of God to your roots right now, and I cut myself loose from your assignment in Jesus name according to Matthew 3:10!

Almighty God, I come in alignment with your word in Ezekiel 26:9. Every demonic wall that has been erected against my marriage, ministry, calling, I use the axe of God to break down your towers and shatter into pieces your strongholds! I decree that you will become rubble before my eyes! I declare you will be transported to ravaged places where the fire of God will consume you to chaff in Jesus name. Amen!

ASSIGNMENT

Study the scripture references.

Write down your own prayer points using the Axe of God.

_____

_____

_____

_____

_____

_____

_____

_____

_____

_____

_____

_____

_____

_____

_____

_____

_____

_____

_____

_____

The Sword of the Spirit

A sword is a weapon with a handle and a long metal blade usually sharpened on both sides, used for striking or thrusting. In the Chapter, *Dressed for Battle,* we looked at how the Roman legions used this weapon in their military campaigns. Their individual and collaborative skill set enabled these warriors to bring nations and kingdoms down to their knees.

The Bible is filled with situations that involve the use a sword. One of the most well known accounts is found in 1 Samuel 17. David after striking down Goliath used the giant's sword to remove his head. In my opinion, the most outstanding reference to a sword in the Bibleis found in Ephesians chapter 6. Paul describes the Word of God as the Sword of the Spirit. It is with this sword we are able to sever evil connections. It is with this sword we strike the enemy when he attacks our lives. It becomes the weapon of choice when you are in close quarters with Satan or his demons. The prayer points below show how we can engage our enemy when he springs his attacks on us using the sword of the Spirit.

PRAYER POINTS

Hebrews 4:12 (NASB)

"For the word of God is living and active and sharper than any two-edged sword, and piercing as far as the division of soul and spirit, of both joints and marrow, and able to judge the thoughts and intentions of the heart."

Revelation 2:16 (NASB)

'Therefore repent; or else I am coming to you quickly, and I will make war against them with the sword of my mouth."

Ezekiel 21: 9-10 (KJV)

"Son of man, prophesy, and say, thus saith the L*ORD; Say, a sword, a sword is sharpened and also furbished: It is sharpened to make a sore slaughter..."*

Ephesians 6: 17 (KJV)

"...and the sword of the Spirit, which is the word of God."

Father, I decree and declare that your Word, which is your very own self, according to St John 1:1, is my sword. I have been misjudged, misguided, misrepresented, trampled on, and left to die without just cause. I use the Sword of the Spirit to cut off the head of Goliath in Jesus name! I subpoena every Goliath will come up and face me now in this battle. I come to you in no other name but the name of the Lord. I wield the Sword of the Spirit. I command your head to fall to the ground and vultures come and consume your body. Father, let your sword pierce through every wicked spirit and locate the heart filled with evil intention to overthrow and malign me in Jesus name! Great God, fight against them who fight against me! Take hold of shield and buckler and stand up for my help. Almighty Father, sharpen your sword as never before and disfigure every evil spirit sent to destroy me. I use the sword to cut away every generational sickness of hypertension, diabetes, cancer, heart failure, arthritis, memory loss and sudden death from my bloodline. I cut the silver cord with the sword of every witch that goes astral travelling, and I declare that you will not return to your body. I use the sword to cut away every enemy combatant blocking the pathway to my breakthrough. I execute every spirit of lies, deception, envy and strife with the sword of the Lord. I declare a great slaughter in Jesus name. Amen!

ASSIGNMENT

Study the scripture references. Write down your own prayer points using the Sword of the Spirit.

_____

_____

_____

_____

_____

_____

_____

_____

_____

_____

_____

_____

_____

_____

_____

_____

_____

_____

_____

_____

_____

_____

_____

_____

The Breath of God

Breath is the power of breathing air in and out. In the Hebrew language, the word *"ruach"* means wind, breath or spirit. In Genesis 1:2 it was the Spirit of God (*Ruach Elohim*) that moved upon the face of the waters. In Genesis 6:17, the same word translates to "breath of life," and in Genesis 8:1 it is translated "wind".

In other parts of the scriptures, the breath of the Lord is used in the judgment of God's enemies. The verses listed below in the prayer points are some examples of these. The common thread in all these references is that God is dealing with an enemy directly and most severely. Some of these passages talk about God's anger in conjunction with the release of His breath. This breath is not sent to be helpful, beneficial, or creative in these instances. The purpose for the release talked about here is for destruction, desolation, and the total routing of God's enemies. Get this! Everything and everyone that opposes our relationship with Christ to the point that they seek to destroy it is an enemy.

When we come upon stiff resistance from Satan or his agents, ask God to release His breath and blow on them. Ask our Heavenly Father to blow on every evil plantation in or around our lives and declare like Isaiah, that they shall scarcely be planted. God's breath will cause them to wither away and the storms will move them as stubble.

PRAYER POINTS

Job 4:9 (NASB)

"By the breath of God they perish, and by the blast of His anger, they come to an end.

Isaiah 40:24 (ESV)

"Scarcely have they been planted, scarcely have they been sown, scarcely has their stock taken root in the earth, But He merely blows on them, and they wither, And the storm carries them away like stubble."

2 Thessalonians 2:8 (NASB)

"Then that lawless one will be revealed whom the Lord will slay with the breath of His mouth and bring to an end by the appearance of His coming";

Job 26:13 (NASB)

"By His breath, the heavens are cleared; His hand has pierced the fleeing serpent."

Ezekiel 21:31 (NASB)

"I will pour out my indignation on you; I will blow on you with the fire of My wrath, and I will give you into the hand of brutal men, skilled in destruction."

Jehovah, El-Gibor, I ask that you rise in your anger and blow your breath upon every witch, warlock, and evil doer that has been plotting against my life in Jesus name! By your breath, overthrow every territorial witch and wizard that operates in the community of my home, church, and place of work and whereever I go to conduct my personal affairs!

I speak that they will perish, be brought to confusion and stripped of their powers. Let them perish at one blast of your anger in Jesus name! Father, blow on them and cause their powers to wither away. I call forth the power of the Holy Ghost to carry them away as stubble. Jehovah, slay them with the breath of your mouth and end their evil assignments. Father, let none escape your power. I declare that your breath will pierce every fleeing serpent. Father, pour out your indignation and blow your wrath mingled with your fire upon them. Lord, give them over to brutal men skilled in destruction in Jesus name. Amen!

ASSIGNMENT

Study the scripture references. Write down your own prayer points using the Breath of God.

_____

_____

_____

_____

_____

_____

_____

_____

_____

_____

_____

_____

_____

_____

_____

_____

_____

_____

_____

_____

The Finger of God

The finger is the part of the hand used for writing, touching or holding things. It has a range of motions that enable various tasks to be carried out. Of all our fingers, the two that are most important are the thumb and the index. In Judges 1:6-8, the Bible gives an account of a ruler who had his thumb and great toe removed. Adoni-bezek in his power subdued 70 territories. When he conquered them, he removed the great toes and thumbs of the leaders. This was a strategic move as this made these kings handicap. They would never be able to set themselves in battle array or wield a sword again.

In our interactions, the index finger is the most used when communicating. If police ask a person to point out an offender, they will most likely use their index finger. If a person is making a strong point in a discourse, they use their index finger in gestures. These gestures are a demonstration of sorts projecting authority.

In the book of Daniel, God's finger appeared before the king and his nobles while they were feasting. King Belshazzar invoked the judgment of

Lord when he asked to use God's holy vessels from the temple in Jerusalem in his revellings. The finger that most likely appeared writing on the wall against the king was the index finger. The Finger of God in this application speaks of the judgement of the Lord against something, in the case of King Belshazzar, someone. When we need the Lord to judge a matter or a situation that is adverse to our spiritual development in righteousness, ask the Lord to write against it with his finger. The prayer point that follows gives an illustration of this.

PRAYER POINTS

Exodus 8:19 (KJV)

"Then the magicians said unto Pharaoh, This is the finger of God: and Pharaoh's heart was hardened, and he hearkened not unto them; as the LORD had said."

Luke 11:20 (KJV)

"But if I with the finger of God cast out devils, no doubt the kingdom of God is come upon you."

Daniel 5:5-6 (KJV)

"In the same hour came forth fingers of a man's hand, and wrote over against the candlestick upon the plaster of the wall of the king's palace: and the king saw the part of the hand that wrote. Then the king's countenance was changed, and his thoughts troubled him so that the joints of his loins were loosed, and his knees smote one against another."

Abba Father, Great God, King of kings, Lord of lords. I call forth the Finger of God to appear before any spirit on a mission to steal my blessing and to prevent the flow of God's divine favour in my life. Let their hearts be hardened like Pharaoh to show forth your glory and praise! I command every devil to be thrown out of my life by the Finger of God! I declare that wherever you are hiding, the Finger of God will chase you out of my life in Jesus name! Almighty God, write against every blessing stealer in my surroundings. Lord Jesus, cause their countenance to change before my eyes. Let them become troubled and tormented by their evil thoughts towards me.

I decree that their loins will be loosed and their knees give way. I prophesy that fear and terror will grip their hearts until they let go of what rightfully belongs to me. I command every spirit that has swallowed my blessings to cough them up by the Finger of God. Lord Jesus, point out every external enemy that is determined to assassinate my character. Bring to an open shame every undermining spirit operating in the church and the workplace that attacks me in secret and then publicly praises me. Father, cast out of my life every negative word spoken against me. Dismantle every Pharaoh spirit that oppresses me. I adjure the spirit of Jezebel to become inoperable by the Finger of God. I declare that the kingdom of God is for me, is within me and around me. I decree that I am unstoppable and unmovable in Jesus name Amen!

ASSIGNMENT

Study the scripture references. Write down your own
prayer points using the Finger of God.

The Right Hand of God

The hand is part of the body that the fingers are connected to; it extends from arm. These two parts of our body are arguably the most used, outside of the heart, that never stops. Our eyes will see, but it is the hand that reaches. Our stomach gets hungry, however, it is the hand that takes food to the mouth so we are fed. Our hands, simply put, makes everyday life easier to navigate.

In the Bible, the right hand is used metaphorically to mean honour and strength (might). An example of honour is *"The Lord said unto my Lord, Sit thou at my right hand, until I make thine enemies thy footstool,"* (Psalms 110: 1). The right hand here signifies the place of honour. David saw Christ prophetically taking His seat beside God the Father after His atoning sacrifice on earth. God the Father had the Son to sit at the place of honour until He subdued all things under Him. An example of strength or might is *"Thy right hand, O Lord, is become glorious in power: thy right hand, O Lord, hath dashed in pieces the enemy,"* (Exodus 15:6). Here Moses sings of God's military might against the armies of Egypt after they were drowned in the Red Sea. God's show of His strength destroyed one of the world's superpowers then, in just a few minutes.

As Christian soldiers, we invoke the Right Hand of God when we face forces that are stronger than us. Israel was no match for the Egyptians. However, the Right Hand of God became glorious in power and gave the Egyptians a knock out punch! What is overwhelming you today? Ask God to release His right hand and give that thing a severe blow in Jesus' mighty name!

PRAYER POINTS

Psalm 138:7 (NASB)

"Though I walk in the midst of trouble, You will revive me; You will stretch forth Your hand against the wrath of my enemies, And Your right hand will save me."

Exodus 15:6 (NASB)

"Your right hand, O LORD, is majestic in power, your right hand, O LORD, shatters the enemy."

Exodus 15:12 (ESV)

"You stretched out your right hand; the earth swallowed them."

Psalm 21:8 (ESV)

"Your hand will find out all your enemies; your right hand will find out those who hate you."

Psalm 110:1 (NASB)

"The LORD says to my Lord: "Sit at My right hand until I make your enemies a footstool for your feet."

Father, daily my enemies rise against me with vengeance. They have been multiplying at high speed. This battle is bigger than me, so I turn it over to you, Jesus. Lord stretch forth your right hand against the wrath of my enemies and cause their anger to subside in Jesus name! Mighty God, deliver me by your right hand. Abba Father, your word reminds me that your right hand is majestic in power and it shatters the enemy. Now great God, raise your right hand and smash to pieces the enemies of my mind, soul, and body in Jesus name! Lord, stretch forth your right hand and let the earth swallow up all my enemies that are too strong for me. Father, those who pretend to love me but are spewing out the venom of hatred, let your right hand find them out and bring their masquerade to a halt. Jehovah, I announce to principalities and powers that I sit in heavenly places. I decree that my enemies are now my footstool and this will become their permanent position in Jesus' Name! Father, give them a knockout punch with your right hand! Cause them to become permanently unconscious and never to rise to power in Jesus name. Amen!

ASSIGNMENT

Study the scripture references. Write down your own prayer points using the Right Hand of God.

_____

_____

_____

_____

_____

_____

_____

_____

_____

_____

_____

_____

_____

_____

_____

_____

_____

_____

_____

_____

_____

_____

_____

The Wind of God

Wind is the natural movement of air at a certain velocity moving in a particular direction. Throughout history, the devastating effects of wind at high velocity have been well documented. From the severe desert storms in places like the Sahara, to the mighty and powerful hurricanes and tornados in the Americas, wind power is an awesome power to behold.

As mighty as the wind systems on earth are, none can compare to those that God himself employs to show His glory. Can you imagine the sight at the Red Sea when the children of Israel saw God's wind blow a path in a great body of water that prevented them from escaping the might of Pharaoh's army? The water parted and formed a path in the middle of the sea that was dry. In other words, there were no mud puddles to bog down the people of God as they made their escape from Pharaoh. Even more amazing, was Israel witnessed the Egyptians trying to pursue them and God's intervention: causing the pathway to close up and drowned the entire army of a world superpower.

Wind also provides energy. Early sailors used this energy to move great ships across huge oceans in order to discover new lands and opportunities. Today, we use wind to generate electric energy to power our homes and businesses. As believers, sometimes we get stuck at place or in a season of drought for too long. It is in these places and seasons we ask God to release His wind for propulsion and promotion. When God releases His winds of favour, buckle up for your next season of breakthrough.

Deliverance is at hand! Satan, just like the Egyptian slave master, is always looking to recapture former slaves of sin. We were once former slaves to sin mainly because we were born in sin. However, we have been set free through the work of Christ on Calvary's cross. When the enemy of our soul corners us at our "Red Sea", we need to pray the God of our salvation for the release of His wind. This will make a way of escape and drown the enemy that has cornered us. Glory be to God for His awesome power to save!

PRAYER POINTS

Exodus 15:10 (NASB)

"You blew with your wind, the sea covered them; they sank like lead in the mighty waters."

Exodus 10:19 (NASB)

"So the LORD shifted the wind to a very strong west wind which took up the locusts and drove them into the Red Sea; not one locust was left in all the territory of Egypt."

2 Samuel 22:16 (NASB)

"Then the channels of the sea appeared, the foundations of the world were laid bare by the rebuke of the LORD, at the blast of the breath of His nostrils."

Psalm 78:26 (NASB)

"He caused the east wind to blow in the heavens, and by His power, He directed the south wind."

Exodus 14:21-22 (NASB)

"Then Moses stretched out his hand over the sea, and the LORD swept the sea back by a strong east wind all night and turned the sea into dry land, so the waters were divided. The sons of Israel went through the midst of the sea on the dry land, and the waters were like a wall to them on their right hand and on their left."

Father, in the mighty name of Jesus Christ, I thank you that you possess victory! You are my portion in the land of the living. Lord, I pray to you now in the name of Jesus Christ of Nazareth that you will release your wind to blow away every inhibitor in my life! Let every "Red Sea" that separates me from moving toward my promise land be parted by your East wind in the mighty name of Jesus Christ!

Let the blast of your nostrils expose every demonic foundation in my life in the name of Jesus. Father, remove every locust eating up my victories and substance. Let your West wind remove them in the mighty name of Jesus. Great God! Direct the South wind of your power in my life today and remove all obstacles to spiritual growth in the mighty name of Jesus. Father, make a path of dry land for me through every sea that forms a blockade to my success in the name of Jesus. I thank you now, Father that your winds of favor are now propelling me into my next season. I decree that I shall have good success in the mighty name of Jesus Christ. Amen!

ASSIGNMENT

Study the scripture references. Write down your own prayer points using the wind of God.

_____

_____

_____

_____

_____

_____

_____

_____

_____

_____

_____

_____

_____

_____

_____

_____

_____

_____

_____

_____

The Arrows of God

An arrow is straight, pointed, projectile created to be shot from a bow in the hands of a trained warrior. This weapon was used with deadly accuracy in ancient times. One of my favorite movie scenes where the bow and arrow is used is from the movie, *300*. In this scene, the Persians are trying to invade Greece and have met up on King Leonidas I and his coalition of Greek soldiers. A messenger from the Persian king, Xerxes, threatens the Greeks saying their armies' arrows will blot out the sun. In the scene that follows, a multitude of arrows come down on the Greek army from the Persian camp. The sheer number of those arrows blocked the sun light out (according to the movie of course).

Earlier I made mention that defending forces would use fiery arrows to repel the advances of invading forces against their cities. Skilled archers would be positioned on the walls to lay down a barrage of arrows to either push back or stop the invaders dead in their tracks. On the open battlefield, the arrow was used as a long-range projectile to take the main sting out of an enemy's attack. It was also use to scatter army formations and expose vulnerabilities.

As stated before, Satan's attacks are mostly in close quarters. The enemy of our soul seeks to get near to us to do his damage. However, we have to use the long-range effects of the Arrows of God to weaken the devil and his forces so by the time they get near us the main sting is taken out of their attack. Therefore, when Satanic forces are in battle array against us we invoke the Arrows of God to scatter and discombobulate them. When this is done, they are now easy target for prayer warriors to come in and finish off. So before the enemy causes you to unsheath The Sword of the Spirit (the Word of God), hit him from a distance with the Arrows of God.

PRAYER POINTS

2 Kings 13:17 (NASB)

"And he said, Open the window eastward. And he opened it. Then Elisha said, Shoot. And he shot. And he said, The arrow of the Lord's deliverance, and the arrow of deliverance from Syria: for thou shalt smite the Syrians in Aphek, till thou have consumed them."

Psalm 64:7-10 (NASB)

"But God will shoot at them with an arrow; suddenly they will be wounded. So they will make him stumble; their own tongue is against them; all who see them will shake the head. Then all men will fear, and they will declare the work of God and will consider what He has done."

2 Samuel 22:15 (NASB)

"And He sent out arrows, and scattered them, lightning, and routed them."

Psalm 7:13 (NASB)

"He has also prepared for himself deadly weapons; He makes His arrows fiery shafts."

Psalm 18:14 (NASB)

"He sent out His arrows, and scattered them and lightning flashes in abundance, and routed them."

Father, in the mighty name of Jesus Christ, I come to You today! You are great and greatly to be praised! As I enter into this sphere of warfare today, I am asking you to make ready your arrows against all intrinsic and extrinsic enemies. Father, shoot your arrow and scatter them, let the arrow of your deliverance wound the enemy of my destiny. In the mighty name of Jesus Christ, let every enemy in and around my life be stricken sore with the Arrows of God.

Father, prepare your fiery darts against the devil, his host and every demonic army arrayed against my family, brethren, mission, and ministry! Let the arrows of the LORD repel every diabolical advance against my life, call, family, finances, health, dreams and aspirations in the mighty name of Jesus Christ! Let every opposition against godly promotions in my life be utterly consumed by the fiery Arrows of God. Father, rain terror in the camp of all demonic saboteurs in the name of Jesus Christ! Let every Satanic hand holding any area of my life be pierced by the Arrow of God in Jesus' mighty name. Father, thank you for the victory. Amen!

ASSIGNMENT

Study the scripture references. Write down your own prayer points using the Arrows of God.

_____

_____

_____

_____

_____

_____

_____

_____

_____

_____

_____

_____

_____

_____

_____

_____

_____

_____

_____

_____

_____

_____

The Lightning
& Thunder of God

Lightning is an electrostatic spark or discharge that usually occurs in a thunder or electric storm. Thunder is a loud noise produced by rapidly expanding air heated by a lightning discharge.

One of the most terrible occurrences in the elements under the heavens is a thunderstorm. Thunderstorms are a remarkable sight to see; huge flashes of lighting followed by loud claps of thunder send even grown men hiding. This awesome display of power is capable of bringing entire regions to a halt, as venturing outside becomes very dangerous. During the course of human history, there have been many incidents of persons and objects electrocuted during a storm. There are documented cases of rocks and trees literally being shattered as

if processed in a grinding machine. Lightning and thunder are very dangerous!

Thunderstorms in the physical world are mighty. What about those in the spiritual realm? God made them both, and if the ones we see cause us to quake, then what about the ones angels and demons see. I am sure when God releases them Satan and his host have to move. So how then do we employ the lighting and thunder of the Lord in spiritual warfare? We learned earlier that lighting strikes not only electrocute, but also shatter objects. When Satanic forces have amassed themselves against you or your family, when works of darkness have cemented themselves in areas of your proclivities and are determined not to let go, when Satanic agents namely witches and warlocks are working against you from their evil altars, it is then you need to invoke the Lightning and Thunder of God to drive fear in to demonic armies, shatter evil works, and strike evil practitioners working against you. See how in the prayer points that follow.

PRAYER POINTS

Exodus 19:16 (NASB)

"So it came about on the third day, when it was morning, that there were thunder and lightning flashes and a thick cloud upon the mountain and a

very loud trumpet sound so that all the people who were in the camp trembled."

Exodus 20:18 (NASB)

"All the people perceived the thunder and the lightning flashes and the sound of the trumpet and the mountain smoking; and when the people saw it, they trembled and stood at a distance."

Revelation 16:18 (NASB)

"And there were flashes of lightning and sounds and peals of thunder; and there was a great earthquake, such as there had not been since man came to be upon the earth, so great an earthquake was it, and so mighty."

Psalm 97:4 (NASB)

"His lightning lit up the world; The earth saw and trembled."

Father, in the mighty name of Jesus, today I ask that you release your thunder and lightning in the atmosphere to scatter my enemies. Let the fear of God rest upon them, and cause them to tremble uncontrollably. Every stubborn problem in my life I command you now to receive the Lightning and Thunder of God in the mighty name of Jesus Christ. Almighty God, strike every demonic stronghold in my life and route them out in Jesus name. Let the Lightning and Thunder of God shatter all Satanic embargo on my life, ministry and mission in the name of Jesus Christ!

May the Lightning and Thunder of your presence quake in my life and break up every dead work in Jesus' mighty name. Oh Lord, send your thunder and hail against every pharaoh in my life in the name of Jesus Christ! Father, let my adversaries be broken in pieces. Thunder against them in the heavens according to your word in 1 Samuel 2:10. Abba Father, let your voice thunder against every setback, mediocrity, and satanic delay in my life, family, church, and community in the mighty name of Jesus Christ! Father, I receive victory from you now. Thank you in Jesus' mighty name. Amen!

ASSIGNMENT

Study the scripture references. Write down your own prayer points using the Lightning and Thunder of God.

_____

_____

_____

_____

_____

_____

_____

_____

_____

_____

_____

_____

_____

_____

_____

_____

_____

_____

_____

_____

The Fire of God

Fire is a state, process, or instance of combustion. It is the process in which fuel is ignited, combined with oxygen, giving off light, heat, and flame. Fire is arguably the most used form of energy in human society. We use fire to power our machines; we use fire for cooking, heating, and to produce electricity just to name a few. Therefore, fire is very important to humankind. Fire is also very dangerous, and much care ought to be taken when using it. One wrong move and the thing that brings so much benefit can cause great damage.

Out in California, wildfires cost the state millions of dollars in damage each year. The human cost is even greater. Lives, livelihood, and homes are consumed and turned to ash. In cities around the world where living quarters are very close, a single spark could destroy an entire building, causing death and displacing many individuals.

The Bible tells us, "God is a consuming fire" (Hebrews 12:29). Therefore, we ought to revere Him. In the book of Exodus, God appears to Moses in the form of a scrub on fire. I bet it was amazing for Moses to see the intense fire, but not see the bush being consumed. Maybe Moses questioned himself, "How could such flames be so intense yet the bush looks as fresh and green as any would after morning dew or rain?" God is infinitely more awesome and powerful in His appearance or manifestations by fire. My friend, that same fire that rested so gently on the flower on the backside of the mountain is able to burn out and totally eradicate Satanic infestations. It is also able to purge the character of man. Just ask Isaiah who got a tongue purging by it.

The Fire of God will give you righteous warmth and comfort all while scourging the wicked one and his agents. When you need to set Satanic forces on fire so that they release their hold, we invoke the Fire of God. When Satanic forces need to be pushed back or their battle lines broken, set in disarray, we need to invoke the Fire of God. Indeed a fire goes before Him and burns up all His enemies round about! Let us call down holy fire from heaven in Jesus' mighty name.

PRAYER POINTS

Hebrews 12:28 & 29 (KJV)

"Wherefore we receiving a kingdom which cannot be moved, let us have grace, whereby we may serve God acceptably with reverence and godly fear: For our God is a consuming fire."

Psalms 97:3 (KJV)

"A fire goeth before him, and burneth up his enemies round about."

Genesis 19:24 (KJV)

"Then the Lord rained upon Sodom and upon Gomorrah brimstone and fire from the Lord out of heaven"

Exodus 9:24 (KJV)

"So there was hail, and fire mingled with the hail, very grievous, such as there was none like it in all the land of Egypt since it became a nation."

Exodus 13:21 (KJV)

"And the Lord went before them by day in a pillar of a cloud, to lead them the way; and by night

in a pillar of fire, to give them light; to go by day and night."

1 Kings 18:38 (KJV)

"Then the fire of the Lord fell and consumed the burnt sacrifice, and the wood, and the stones, and the dust, and licked up the water that was in the trench."

My Heavenly Father, I come to you in no other name but the name of Jesus Christ, your only begotten son. I honour you as my God, and give you all glory, honour, and praise! I acknowledge that Jesus Christ is my Lord, King, God, and Savior. Father, your word tells me that you are a consuming fire. Let your fire now move through my life and burn out all evil plantations in Jesus' mighty name! Let your fire burn up all enemies of the cross of Jesus Christ.

Let your fire destroy all intrinsic and extrinsic enemies in my life in Jesus mighty name. Father, lead me by your pillar of cloud and fire as I travel through every spiritual wilderness in the name of Jesus Christ! Let the Holy Ghost fire burn from the crown of my head to the soul of my feet in the name of Jesus Christ. Let the Holy Ghost fire burn out all uncleanness in my bloodline in the name of Jesus.

LORD, let your fire be very grievous against all demonic opposition to my ministry in the mighty name of Jesus Christ. Father, vex them sore and overthrow their works. Father, rule in my heart and let your consuming fire overflow into every area of my being in Jesus' mighty name! Father, send your fire down from heaven and prove to every prophet of Baal opposing me that you are the only God and there is none other! I thank you now for hearing me in the name of Jesus Christ I pray. Amen!

ASSIGNMENT

Study the scripture references. Write down your own prayer points using the Fire of the God.

_____

_____

_____

_____

_____

_____

_____

_____

_____

_____

_____

_____

_____

_____

_____

_____

_____

_____

_____

_____

_____

_____

The Hailstones of God

Hailstones are chunks of ice that fall from the clouds. This form of precipitation occurs mainly in cold weather. These blocks of ice do great damage and can cause death to animals and humans. I often joke about my fellow citizens' ability to find and hurl stones. When Jamaicans fought back in the days, it would always amaze me how we were able to find and hurl stones with great accuracy.

I remember witnessing a high school football (soccer) game that turned into a brawl. I recall seeing stones thrown everywhere. You recall from my earlier statement about the scene in *300* where the Persian king's messenger stated that his army's arrows would block out the sun? Well that day at my high school the sky was filled with stones! I remember my younger brother and I ran, securing ourselves from danger. While exiting the compound, I saw a football player from the visiting school, get hit in the back with a stone.

One of the threats that Jamaicans love to issue when provoked is, "Mi wee buss yuh head enuh." In proper English, "I will burst your head." Usually this is done by tossing a stone in the direction of the target. By no means am I advocating violence; but the stone was the weapon against the enemy.

As believers, we can wage a good warfare by using the Hailstones of God. We must not be terrified to release hailstones into the camp of the enemy. We can also pray and ask God to let torrential hailstones fall upon the head of our enemy and destroy satanic stronghold in our lives. Christian warriors, we must always take advantage of the long-range weapons in our arsenal. Do not wait until Satan gets close to home. Hit him while he is at a distance!

PRAYER POINTS

Joshua 10:11 (KJV)

"As they fled from before Israel, while they were at the descent of Beth-horon, the LORD threw large stones from heaven on them as far as Azekah, and they died; there were more who died from the hailstones than those whom the sons of Israel killed with the sword."

Job 38 22-23 (KJV)

"Hast thou entered into the treasures of the snow? or hast thou seen the treasures of the hail, which I have reserved against the time of trouble, against the day of battle and war?"

Psalm 105:32 (KJV)

"He gave them hail for rain And flaming fire in their land."

Exodus 9:23 (KJV)

"Moses stretched out his staff toward the sky, and the LORD sent thunder and hail, and fire ran

down to the earth. And the LORD rained hail on the land of Egypt."

Father, you are sovereign, and I trust you. Almighty God, I beseech you to take up shield and butler and stand up for my help. Lord cause the heavens to release huge hailstones into the camp of every enemy pursuing me. Let the hailstones of God destroy all evil plantations in my life in Jesus name! Let your hailstones mix with your thunder and rain; scatter every enemy that is too strong for me. Father, annihilate their places of operation and their satellites in Jesus Name! Oh Lord, release the treasures of your hail against every Satanic altar. Be assaulted and completed destroyed in the mighty name of Jesus Christ. Lord, rain terror into the camp of every evil army coming against me in the mighty name of Jesus! Frustrate them with your hailstones. Jehovah Gibbor, arise in your power, oh Lord, and overthrow them! Thank you, Lord, for the victory in Jesus' mighty name. Amen!

ASSIGNMENT

Study the scripture references. Write down your own prayer points using the Hailstones of God.

_____

_____

_____

_____

_____

_____

_____

_____

_____

_____

_____

_____

_____

_____

_____

_____

_____

_____

_____

_____

_____

_____

The Earthquake of the Lord

A sudden and violent shaking of the ground, earthquakes can sometimes cause significant destruction and devastation. When they occur underwater, they can cause tsunamis.

Without a doubt, an earthquake is the most powerful of all natural disasters. They happen without warning, no clue or queue, just vibration and destruction in seconds! Earthquakes can trigger mass fires and flooding. When an earthquake occurs near coastal regions, huge volumes of water in the form of tsunamis move inland, resulting in the flooding of coastal cities or towns. In dense urban areas, the rupture of gas lines and underground electrical cables can result in fires. In Fukushima, Japan in 2016 an earthquake caused the disruption of a nuclear power plant resulting in the evacuation of residents from the areas around the plant.

In scripture, God caused the earth to swallow up some men who rebelled against Moses' leadership. In Numbers 16, we find the account of this event. I can just imagine how frightening this was. Korah and his companions were questioning the call of God on Moses and Aaron. Before you knew it, the earth gave way beneath them and they were no more. God buried them alive and caused great fear to come over those who would dear question His choice of Moses and Aaron as leaders of Israel. Even though the Bible did not explicitly state that an earthquake occurred, I am positive that some movement of the earth took place enough to prevent Korah and his 250 followers from escaping a sure judgment. In the New Testament, Paul and Silas were delivered from imprisonment by an earthquake that shook the very foundation of the prison. The Earthquake of the Lord even caused chains and fetters to fall off his chosen vessels, held for preaching the Gospel of Jesus Christ. So terrifying was the event and complete was the deliverance that the jailers were about to kill themselves. However, notice the power of God here. Even though the other prisoners were free, none had the audacity to escape. I often wondered why? Could it be the shock of what just happened? Only an interview with one of these men. or a revelation from the Holy Spirit could confirm that. The persons that God showed up for were set free and able, by God's grace, to preach salvation to the chief jailer and his family.

When we face the enemy of our calling who has his entourage of accusers assembled against us, or when we face imprisonment by Satanic agents trying to stop us from the work of the Lord, we call on our Heavenly Father to release His earthquake to shake the ground beneath our enemy's feet and swallow them up. We can use the Earthquake of God to destroy foundational problems in our generation and to release prison doors.

PRAYER POINTS

Acts 16:26 (KJV)

"Suddenly there was a great earthquake, so that the very foundations of the prison were shaken; and at once all the doors were opened, and everyone's shackles were unfastened."

Isaiah 29:6 (KJV)

"You shall be visited and delivered by the Lord of hosts with thunder and earthquake and great noise, with whirlwind and tempest and the flame of a devouring fire."

Matthew 28:2 (KJV)

"And, behold, there was a great earthquake: for the angel of the Lord descended from heaven, and came and rolled back the stone from the door, and sat upon it."

Heavenly Father, I worship you and praise your holy name as I come to you today! Father, I come in no other name but the name of Jesus Christ, your only begotten Son. Father, let your earthquake shake every Satanic prison in my life and make all doors in front of me to open at thy shaking. I command every chain to detach itself from me in Jesus Name. Let every evil foundation in my life be destroyed entirely by your earthquake, oh Lord!

Father, visit the enemies of my calling with a vengeance, and wholly overrun them in Jesus mighty name. Let your earthquake shake beneath every evil foot and destabilise them so they cannot efficiently launch any attacks against me. Sovereign Lord, rid my life entirely of every structure that obstructs your power and blessings in Jesus' mighty name.

Let the earth swallow up every Korah spirit that questions your divine call on my life in the mighty name of Jesus Christ. Heavenly Father, thank you for the victory you have given me over the enemy of my soul in Jesus' mighty name. Amen!

ASSIGNMENT

Study the scripture references. Write down your own prayer points using the Earthquake of the Lord.

_____

_____

_____

_____

_____

_____

_____

_____

_____

_____

_____

_____

_____

_____

_____

_____

_____

_____

_____

_____

_____

_____

The Blood of Jesus Christ

Blood is defined as the fluid in the body that circulates through the veins carrying oxygen and nutrients to cell; it also aids in the removal of waste and harmful toxins.

In Christian circles, especially charismatic ones, there is a lot of misunderstanding about how the Blood of Jesus Christ is applied in spiritual warfare. The precious Blood of Jesus Christ first and foremost ransomed us from sin and death. It is the complete appeasement of the wrath of God. It is through the blood of Jesus Christ that we have: redemption (Eph. 1:7); justification (Rom. 5:9); peace with God (Col. 1:20); cleansing from sin (1 John 1:7) and an everlasting covenant with God, our Heavenly Father. It is essential to understand that Jesus Christ is our High Priest. Just as how the high priest on earth went into the Holy of Holies and presented the blood of animals upon the altar, so in like manner, Jesus Christ entered heaven (Heb. 9:12) and offered up His blood once and for all for humanity.

So how do we apply the Blood of Jesus Christ in warfare? Shana-Kay and I have seen and heard people casting out demons from people saying things like, "Satan, the blood is against you," or "the blood," or "I plead the blood against you Satan," etc. Let me make it entirely clear this should not be the common practice without having the right understanding of why and when we use the Blood of Jesus. Even though God understands what we are trying to convey, we must be sure to use the Blood of Jesus Christ appropriately. Let us go back to the Old Testament to see just how the Levitical Priesthood used the blood of animals in the various rites of that time.

The list below outlines how the blood of animals was used in the Old Testament (please note that Jesus' blood is used in like manner in the New Testament):

1. **To protect the people of God from the death angel** (Exodus 12:13)
2. **To seal God's covenant with His people** (Exodus 24:8)
3. **To sanctify the High Priest, his sons, and their garments** (Leviticus 8:30)

4. **To make atonement for sins** (Leviticus 17:11)

5. **To sanctify the place and articles of worship** (Hebrews 9:21-22)

6. **To sanctify God's people** (Hebrews 10:10)

In the list above, please note that the blood was always placed on people or things that God wanted to separate to Himself, protect from destruction and for the making of atonement for sin. The Blood of Jesus Christ, therefore, should be placed on one's self, our family, our possessions. Jesus Christ uses His blood in the cleansing of our sins (*It is the blood of the New Testament*). In spiritual warfare, the Blood of Jesus Christ, therefore, **covers** the believer, so we are not under God's wrath, thereby removing Satan's legal rights to attack or accuse the believer. It speaks for the believer, attesting to the truth that the full demand of God was met in Jesus' sacrificial offering.

Therefore, the next time you enter the realm of spiritual warfare be sure to apply the precious Blood of Jesus Christ over your life, your family, friends, and over the things that you possess. **Be sure that you**

confess and repent of sins, and forgive ALL who have offended or hurt you.

I plead the Blood of Jesus Christ! What does this mean? Well a let us look at the word plead. A "plead" is a legal term used to invoke or reference a law to accuse or defend someone. In court, you will hear a judge as this question. How do you plead?

Earlier I indicated that God sits as the supreme Judge of the entire universe. We are the circuit judges. This justice system also has everyone as a defendant before God. Satan stands as the accuser and consistently lays his charges. Jesus Christ is the great advocate and stands ready to defend anyone who enters a plea of His blood. The only way to enter this plea is by surrendering one's live completely to Him. When believers enter this plea Satan's accusation looses merit as the Blood of Jesus activates the tender mercies of God.

So back to my point, when we enter spiritual warfare we have to ensure that we confess our sins, forgive those who sin against us and let go the hurt a pain they caused (casting our cares upon Jesus Christ for He cares for us). This assures us of safety from satanic devices when we engage his forces in battle!

Therefore when you now "plead the Blood of Jesus Christ, do so with the understanding that you invoking the mercies of God for indeed when He sees the Blood He will pass over you!

PRAYER POINTS

Leviticus 17:11 (KJV)

"For the life of the flesh is in the blood: and I have given it to you upon the altar to make an atonement for your souls: for it is the blood that maketh an atonement for the soul."

Exodus 12:13 (KJV)

"And the blood shall be to you for a token upon the houses where ye are: and when I see the blood, I will pass over you, and the plague shall not be upon you to destroy you when I smite the land of Egypt."

John 6:53 (KJV)

"Then Jesus said unto them, Verily, verily, I say unto you, Except ye eat the flesh of the Son of man, and drink his blood, ye have no life in you."

Hebrews 12:24 (KJV)

"And to Jesus the mediator of the new covenant, and to the blood of sprinkling, that speaketh better things than that of Abel."

Hebrews 9:22 (KJV)

"And almost all things are by the law purged with blood, and without shedding of blood is no remission."

Luke 22:19-20 (KJV)

"And he took bread, and gave thanks, and brake it, and gave unto them, saying, This is my body which is given for you: this do in remembrance of me. Likewise also the cup after supper, saying, this cup is the new testament in my blood, which is shed for you."

Almighty God, I thank you for sending your only Son Jesus Christ to die in my stead. I have been redeemed through the shed Blood of Jesus Christ. I declare, Father, that I am standing in the pool of the Blood of Jesus Christ. I speak that the Lord orders my footsteps, and my feet are now like hind's feet. I decree that I run through troops and leap over every demonic wall that has been resurrected against my advancement. By faith, I inject into my body the healing properties of the blood of Jesus Christ to locate and cancel every trace of sickness and disease floating in my body.

I place the blood of Jesus Christ over my life to repel every witchcraft spell, hex, vex, and incantation from those who operate in the spirits of Jezebel, Sanballat, and Tobiah, Belial, Absalom, and Korah in the name of Jesus! Lord Jesus Christ, your blood is one that speaks better things according to Hebrews 12:24. Let your blood, Lord, speak against and repudiate near success-syndrome, failure at the edge of breakthrough, untimely death, accidents, setbacks, demotions, delayed promotions, wrong associations and alliances, lousy decision-making, spiritual drought and dryness, destiny killers, financial lack and leaking pockets, horrible business contracts and negotiations, fear of the unknown, and marital problems. Blood of Jesus Christ, form a barricade around my mind, body, soul and spirit; around my home, marriage, family, place of employment, business ventures and opportunities, in Jesus name. Amen!

ASSIGNMENT

Study the scripture references. Write down your own prayer points using the Blood of Jesus Christ.

_____

_____

_____

_____

_____

_____

_____

_____

_____

_____

_____

_____

_____

_____

_____

_____

_____

_____

_____

_____

Conclusion

The apostle Paul gave an incredible testimony when his mission was coming to an end; he told Timothy that he had fought the good fight, and he had kept the faith. Engage or disengage, whether we like it or not, we are in a spiritual war. From the moment we say "yes" to Jesus Christ our Lord, Satan is seeking to overthrow, defeat, destroy and kill us both physically and spiritually. He is ruthless and will employ different tactics and strategies to annihilate the faithful Saints of Christ. Matthew 11:12 reminds us that, since the days of John the Baptist until the present, the kingdom of heaven suffers violence and the violent take it by force.

Therefore, we have to be empowered to fight the enemy head-on. There is a famous saying, "You don't get what you deserve, but you get what you fight for." Now is the time for the Body of Christ to wake up and ask God to open our spiritual eyes. We have to stop attacking and destroying each other; the real enemy is the devil.

Let us heed the battle cry of the ages, unite under the banner of our Master Jesus Christ. We can no longer settle for the status quo of dressing up going into the four walls of the church and leave feeling defeated. Romans 8:19 makes it clear that the earnest expectation of creation waits for the manifestation of the sons of God. Arise Christian soldiers! Put on the whole armour of God. Use the weapons available to you from this arsenal to claim your possessions and move forward in victory. The battle is not ours but the Lord's!

Acknowledgement

To be successful in the journey of life, one must have the love and support of people. God has steered these special people in our path to help us become all that he wants us to be.

First and foremost, I give extraordinary thanks to our Heavenly Father, Jesus Christ our Lord, and the Blessed Holy Spirit. We give a heartfelt gratitude to our beautiful daughters, Ashandi and Gabrielle Granville, who have endured with us and served as inspiration for us to continue the fight against the enemy.

To our good friends that have impacted our lives and to our spiritual support Minister Jean Fullerton and Pastor Fitzroy Kerr, a big thank you! To our first Editor, Dr Nathan Patrick; second Editor, JWG Publishing (Joan Good); and Graphic Artist, Jae-Anne Willie-Belle, thank you for your kind contribution to the development of Prayer Arsenal.